curious about

ESP

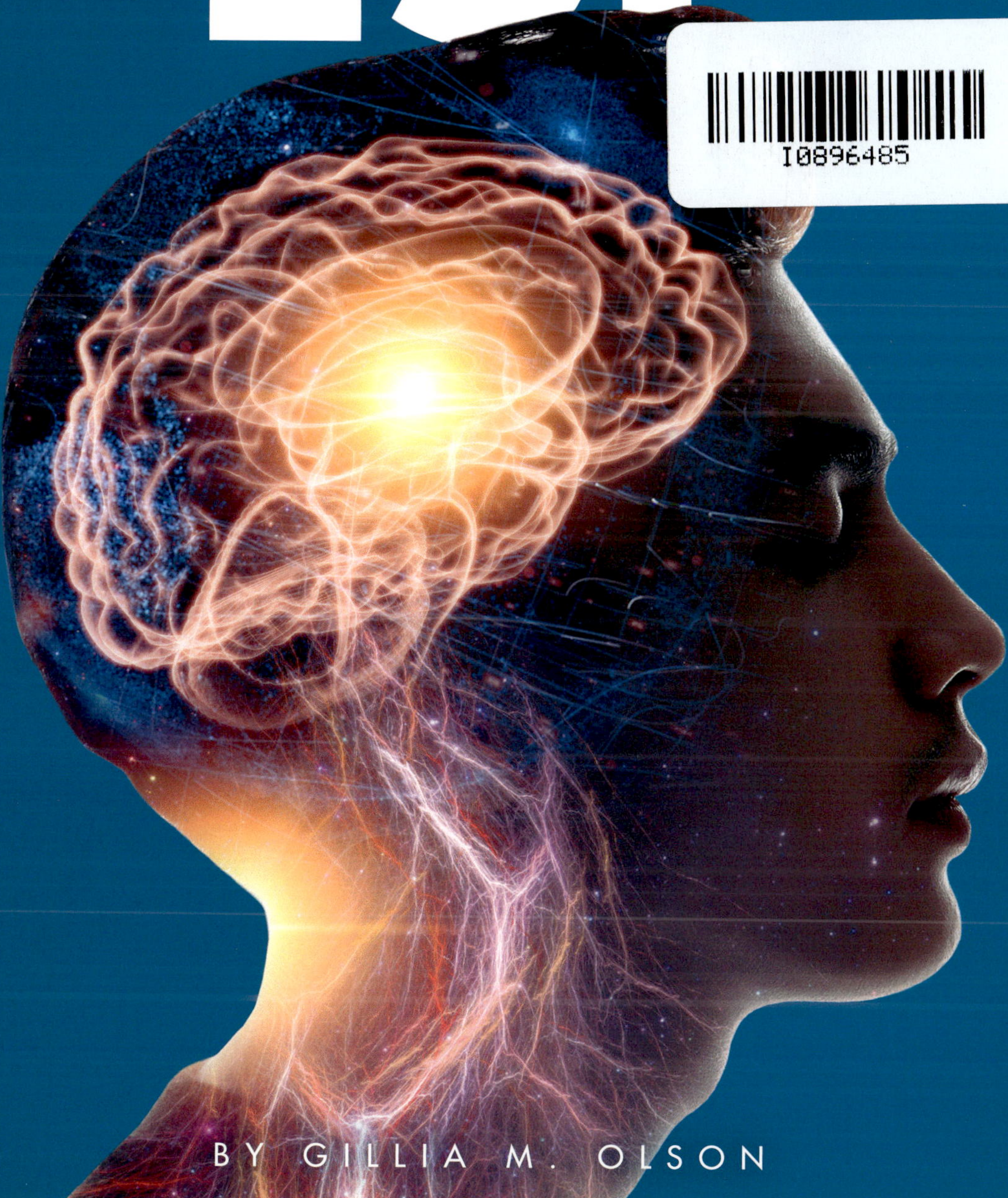

BY GILLIA M. OLSON

AMICUS LEARNING

What are you

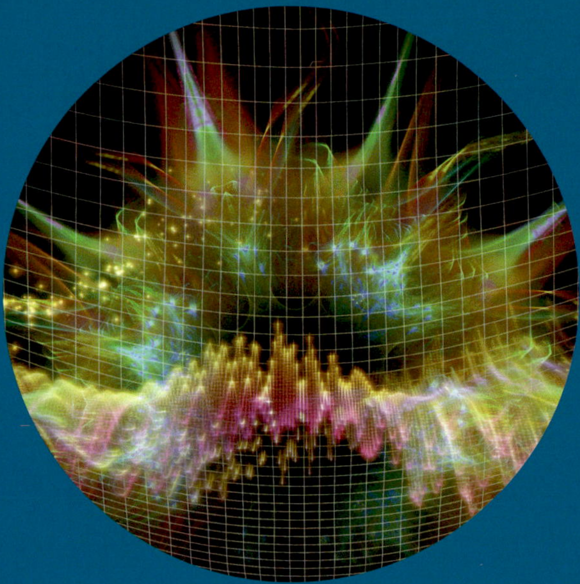

curious about?

CHAPTER THREE

Looking for Answers

PAGE **16**

Curious About is published by
Amicus Learning, an imprint of Amicus
P.O. Box 227
Mankato, MN 56002
www.amicuspublishing.us

Editor: Ana Brauer
Series Designer: Kathleen Petelinsek
Book Designer and Photo Researcher: Emily Dietz

Library of Congress Cataloging-in-Publication Data
Names: Olson, Gillia M., author.
Title: Curious about ESP / by Gillia M. Olson.
Other titles: Curious about extrasensory perception
Description: Mankato, MN : Amicus Learning, an imprint of Amicus, [2025] | Series: Curious about unexplained mysteries | Includes bibliographical references and index. | Audience: Ages 6–9 | Audience: Grades 2–3 | Summary: "Can people really see into the future? Do psychics really have ESP? Learn about the mystery of ESP in this question-and-answer book for elementary-aged readers. Includes infographics, table of contents, glossary, books and websites for further research, and index"— Provided by publisher.
Identifiers: LCCN 2024014751 (print) | LCCN 2024014752 (ebook) | ISBN 9798892000949 (library binding) | ISBN 9798892001526 (paperback) | ISBN 9798892002103 (ebook)
Subjects: LCSH: Extrasensory perception—Juvenile literature. | Psychic ability—Juvenile literature.
Classification: LCC BF1321 .O47 2025 (print) | LCC BF1321 (ebook) | DDC 133.8—dc23/eng/20240424
LC record available at https://lccn.loc.gov/2024014751
LC ebook record available at https://lccn.loc.gov/2024014752

Photos Credits: Alamy Stock Photo/Chroma Collection, 17; Deposit Photos/agsandrew, 2, 6–7; Flickr/Carissa Andrea Thrush, 15 (*second from top*); Getty Images/Laura Cavanaugh, 15 (*bottom*), Michael Kovac, 15 (*middle*), Michael Tullberg, 15 (*top*), Roy Rochlin, 2, 14, Svetlana Repnitskaya, 9; Shutterstock/goffkein.pro, 3, 20–21, Golubovy, 10-11, New Africa, 4–5, Randy Miramontez, 18-19, sutadimages, cover, 1; The Noun Project/ainul muttaqin, 22, 23, Fabien, 22, 23; Wikimedia Commons/Francis Wickware, 16, Sgerbic, 15 (*second from bottom*), Thomas Martin Easterly, 13

Printed in China

CHAPTER ONE

What is ESP?

ESP stands for extrasensory perception. Our five senses are sight, touch, hearing, taste, and smell. "Extrasensory" means beyond the five senses. ESP is also called the sixth sense. People with ESP are called **psychics**.

In movies, psychics are often shown looking through a crystal ball.

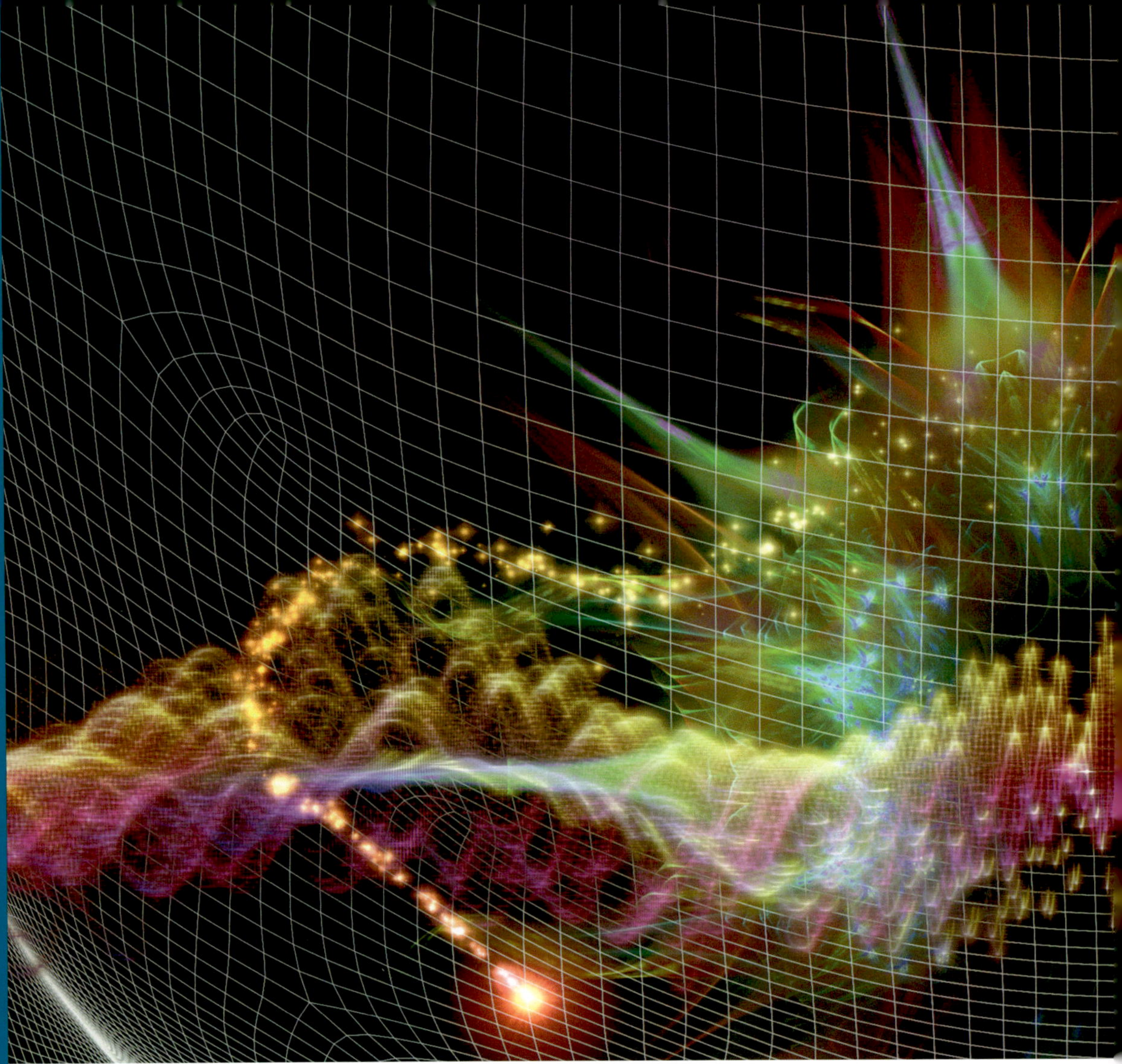

What can psychics do?

Some psychics say they can move things with their minds or see into the past.

There are three kinds of ESP. The first one is **clairvoyance**. It means sensing objects, people, or events other people can't. The second kind is **telepathy**. It means reading minds. The third kind is **precognition**. It means knowing what happens in the future.

Are there other psychic powers?

Some people consider **intuition** to be ESP. Intuition is knowing something, but you don't know why. Maybe you suddenly feel scared. There's no **proof** anything is wrong. But your brain might be picking up clues even if you don't know it.

DID YOU KNOW?

7 out of 10 people feel that there are some things that science can't possibly explain.

Intuition is also called a gut feeling.

CHAPTER TWO

2

Who were the first psychics?

More than 5,000 years ago, Ancient Egyptians tried to talk with the dead. They used a method called scrying. They would drop ink in water. The ink made shapes. People thought the shapes were messages from people who had died.

Ink blots are often used to test people's minds. Not everyone sees the same shapes in the ink.

DID YOU KNOW?

Nearly 4 out of 10 people believe the dead can communicate with the living.

Were there any psychic kids?

In 1848, sisters Maggie and Kate Fox were 14 and 11. They claimed to hear a ghost knocking on walls. Years later, in 1888, Maggie said she and her sister made it up. They cracked their knuckles or toes. That is how they made the knocking sounds.

People believed that the Fox sisters were psychic for many years before Maggie told the truth.

Are there psychics today?

Some people are mediums. They claim they can talk to the dead.

Today, many people claim to be psychics or **mediums**. You can watch TV shows about psychics. Psychics also hold events. The psychics do "readings." They can predict things about the people in the audience.

LONG ISLAND MEDIUM
THERESA CAPUTO

THE DEAD FILES
AMY ALLAN

HOLLYWOOD MEDIUM WITH TYLER HENRY
TYLER HENRY

PSYCHIC KIDS
CHIP COFFEY

CROSSING OVER
JOHN EDWARD

Joseph Rhine believed that someone had ESP if they guessed several of the Zener cards right.

Have real scientists looked into ESP?

Yes, they have. In the 1930s, Joseph Rhine did experiments. He came up with the word "ESP." Rhine used Zener playing cards with symbols. He asked people to guess the symbol. No proof exists for ESP. But that doesn't stop people from believing it is real.

Many people have doubts about Joseph Rhine's tests. They say it would be easy to cheat.

DID YOU KNOW?
Rhine did more than 90,000 experiments in his lifetime.

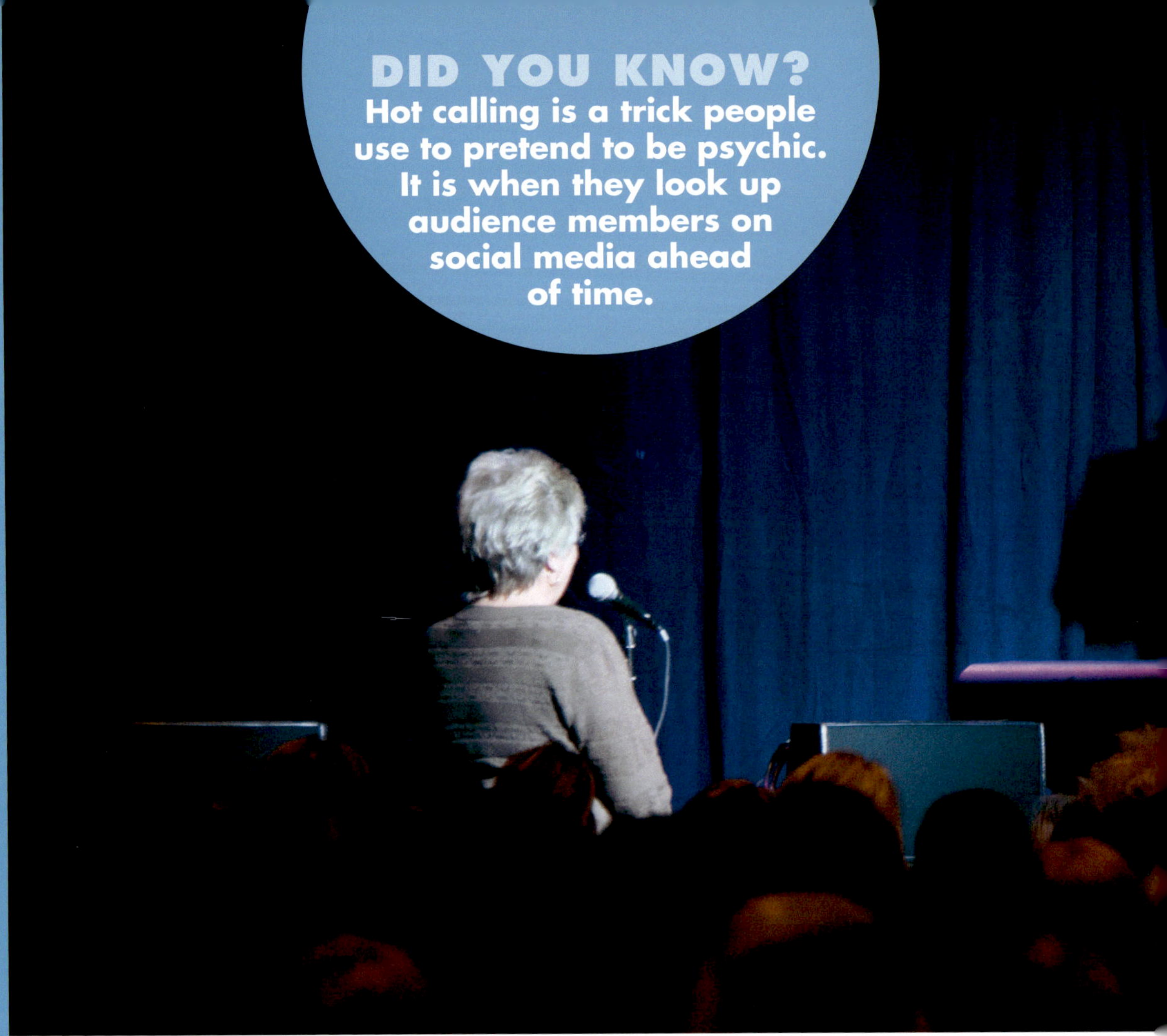

DID YOU KNOW?
Hot calling is a trick people use to pretend to be psychic. It is when they look up audience members on social media ahead of time.

How could you fake ESP?

Some people use the details they read in people's faces to seem psychic.

Cold calling is one trick. A psychic will say something very general. Perhaps they sense an "E" name. In a crowd, someone will have a loved one with an "E" name. Psychics watch people's faces as they talk. A frown means a wrong guess. The psychic then changes what they say.

Why would people try to fake ESP?

Fortune telling and palm readings are common ways psychics can make money.

For money. Psychics get paid for readings. Online readings start at $1 per minute. Famous psychics make millions of dollars. They write books. They sell tickets to shows. Psychics are popular. People are curious about things they can't explain.

STAY CURIOUS!

ASK MORE QUESTIONS

Who are some famous psychics?

What are some other tricks people can use to seem like psychics?

Try a BIG QUESTION: If ESP could be proven real, how would that change your life?

SEARCH FOR ANSWERS

Search the library catalog or the Internet.
A librarian, teacher, or parent can help you.

Using Keywords
Find the looking glass.

Keywords are the most important words in your question.

If you want to know about:

- some famous psychics, type: FAMOUS PSYCHICS
- tricks that psychics might use, type: PSYCHIC TRICKS

LEARN MORE

FIND GOOD SOURCES

Here are some good, safe sources you can use in your research.
Your librarian can help you find more.

Books

ESP by Marysa Storm, 2022.

ESP by Paige V. Polinsky, 2020.

Internet Sites

TED-Ed: Is Telekinesis Real?
https://ed.ted.com/lessons/is-telekinesis-real-emma-bryce
TED-Ed is a non-profit educational site with videos on many topics.

Wonderopolis: Can You Trust Your Intuition?
https://wonderopolis.org/wonder/Can-You-Trust-Your-Intuition
Wonderopolis is a non-profit site for students and their families.

Every effort has been made to ensure that these websites are appropriate for children. However, because of the nature of the Internet, it is impossible to guarantee that these sites will remain active indefinitely or that their contents will not be altered.

SHARE AND TAKE ACTION

Visit your local historical society.
See if any famous psychics lived or practiced in your town.

Watch the body language of your friends and family.
See if you can tell what they are thinking or feeling based on how they carry themselves.

With a trusted adult, visit a psychic.
See what you think for yourself.

GLOSSARY

clairvoyance The ability to sense objects, events, or people other people cannot.

intuition The ability to understand or sense something without knowing why.

medium A person who can talk with the spirits of the dead.

precognition The ability to know something that will happen in the future.

proof Facts or evidence that show something is true.

psychic A person who is sensitive to nonphysical forces.

telepathy The ability to read minds.

INDEX

About the Author

Gillia Olson is a skeptic by nature but loves all things paranormal. She stays curious and open-minded and hopes you will, too. She lives in southern Minnesota.